MY ONE

MY ZONE

DO IT WITH STYLE

ANITA GANERI

EDGE FRANKLIN WATTS

LONDON·SY

FIRST PUBLISHED IN 2010 BY
FRANKLIN WATTS
338 EUSTON ROAD
LONDON NW1 3BH

FRANKLIN WATTS AUSTRALIA
LEVEL 17/207 KENT STREET
SYDNEY NSW 2000

SERIES EDITOR: ADRIAN COLE
ART DIRECTOR: JONATHAN HAIR
DESIGN: BLUE PAW DESIGN
PICTURE RESEARCH: DIANA MORRIS
CONSULTANT: FIONA M. COLLINS,
   ROEHAMPTON UNIVERSITY

A CIP CATALOGUE RECORD OF THIS BOOK
IS AVAILABLE FROM THE BRITISH LIBRARY

ISBN: 978 0 7496 9570 5

DEWEY CLASSIFICATION: 305.2'3'082

ACKNOWLEDGEMENTS:
Titov Andriys/Shutterstock: 28cr. Benis Arapovic/Shutterstock: 36.
Migual Benetez/Rex Features: 16t. Dave M Benett/Getty Images:
11bl. Dean Bertoncelj/Shutterstock: 27bl. John Birdsall/PAI: 43t.
budgetstockphoto/istockphoto: 30br. Diego Cervo/istockphoto: 19.
Brian Chase/Shutterstock: 29cr. Michele Cozzolino/Shutterstock:
28bl. Cross Design/Fotolia: 39. cynoclubs/Shutterstock: 37b. Elena
Elisseeva/Shutterstock: 38. David Fisher /Rex Features: 41bl. Gaye
Gerard/Getty Images: 13bl. Kateryna Govorushchenko/istockphoto:
30l. Grebnev/Shutterstock: 24. Alexander Hafeman/Mlenny
Photography/istockphoto: front cover. Hitdelight/Shutterstock: 28br.
Michael Hoerichs/istockphoto: 9br. hunta/Shutterstock: 25bl. Sajjad
Hussain/AFP/Getty Images: 13tr. ILN/MEPL: 9cl. iofoto/Shutterstock:
42t, 42b. Inga Iranova/istockphoto: 14. Nils Kahle/istockphoto: 23.
Martti Kainulainen/Rex Features: 22. Nicholas Khayat/Enigma/
Rex Features: 16b. Patrick Kovarik/AFP/Getty Images: 12. Rudy K
Lawidjaja/Alamy: 43c. Lepas/Shutterstock: 28cl. Leonard McLane/
Getty Images: 15t. John Miehle/Hulton Archive/Getty Images: 8.
Monkey Business Images /Shutterstock: 35t, 37t. Vishnu Mulakala/
istockphoto: 7bl. Natalya/Shutterstock: 29tr. Nikada/istockphoto:
4, 5. original punkt/Shutterstock: 27tr. parema/istockphoto: 32.
Picturepoint/Topham: 9tr. Pinkcandy/Shutterstock: 34. Popperfoto/
Getty Images: 10. quavondo/istockphoto: 6, 7tr, 18. Trinette Reed/
Shutterstock: 26tl. Rex Features: 40, 43b. Elena Schweitzer/
Shutterstock: 35b. Anna Sedneva/Shutterstock: 31bl. Serg64/
Shutterstock: 29tl. Serhiy /Shutterstock: 25tr. Sinisha/Getty Images:
15b. Sipa Press/Rex Features: 17, 41br. Karel Slavek /Shutterstock:
27cl. studiovespa/istockphoto: 31cl. Kutay Tanir/istockphoto:
33. UPP/Topham: 11tr. Valma Vitaly/Shutterstock: 26b. Wendy
White/Alamy: 20-21. Yannush/Shutterstock: 23b. Peter Zijlstra/
Shutterstock: 31cr.

EVERY ATTEMPT HAS BEEN MADE TO CLEAR COPYRIGHT.
SHOULD THEIR BE ANY INADVERTENT OMISSION PLEASE
APPLY TO THE PUBLISHER FOR RETIFICATION

PRINTED IN CHINA

FRANKLIN WATTS IS A DIVISION OF
HACHETTE CHILDREN'S BOOKS,
AN HACHETTE UK COMPANY.
WWW.HACHETTE.CO.UK

Please note: every effort has been made by the Publishers to ensure that
the websites in this book contain no inappropriate or offensive material.
However, because of the nature of the Internet, it is impossible to
guarantee that the contents of these sites will not be altered. We strongly
advise that Internet access is supervised by a responsible adult.

LOOK OUT FOR...

Words highlighted in the text can be found in the glossary.

*"Hi, welcome to a super-stylish edition of **MY ZONE**. OK, I love shopping and there were so many things to include – we've jam packed this edition until it's fit to burst!"*

Anita x

ALL ABOUT FASHION

Fashion is all about looking good and the kind of clothes you'd love to wear. It's also about style **and the current direction of people's ideas, or trends.**

Your approach to fashion may be to choose your own style, or follow the trends. Either way, you are an individual and free to decide for yourself.

Images of fashion are all around us – whether we follow them or not.

WEBtag

You will see WEBtags throughout this book. Many of the websites feature more information about the articles, videos and up-to-date news and blogs.

Part of looking good includes having the right clothes to suit your style. But it's not just about shopping until you drop. You also need to feel good on the inside – from eating the right things to sleeping well.

Inside you'll find lots of fashion facts, news and behind-the-scenes views, plus things to chat about with your friends. So, whether your style influences are classic Indian (left) or totally **seasonal**, you'll find something to inspire you.

FASHION DECADES

Ever since clothes were first worn, fashions have come and gone. Here's a look back at some of the hottest styles of the last few decades.

1920s

The 'flapper' look was all the rage for women in the 1920s. Dresses were short, sleeveless and loose-fitting. Hairstyles were short and boyish.

1930s

Welcome to the world of the movies! In the 1930s, movie-stars were the fashion **trendsetters**, with glamorous gowns and dramatic make-up.

 This is movie-star Ginger Rogers, wearing an outfit by Bernard Newman in the film *Top Hat* (1935).

1940s

World War II (1939–45) meant nylon for stockings was in short supply. (It was needed to make parachutes.) So women used eyeliner to draw fake seams up the backs of their legs instead.

Sole star billing
by Rayne

CROWN NEOLITE SOLES
Made only by GOODYEAR

1950s

Stiletto shoes were worn for the first time. They had tall, thin, pointed heels which looked like stiletto daggers! They make legs look longer but walking in them is tricky.

Jeans were first worn by factory workers in the USA. In the 1950s, they became popular with teenagers.

www.ftmlondon.org

WEBtag Fashion and Textiles Museum homepage.

9

1960s

Hemlines went up in the 1960s, with the fashion for mini skirts. They were made popular by British designer, Mary Quant, and could even be made from **PVC**.

This is the famous model Twiggy, wearing a mini dress and posing on steps in 1966.

1970s

The 1970s saw trousers with wide, flared bottoms, and shoes with thick, platform soles. They were often worn together, by both men and women.

1980s

Oufits with BIG shoulder pads were popular in the 1980s, as seen in American soaps such as *Dynasty* (right). You needed BIG hair to match, using lots of styling mousse and hairspray.

1990s

In the 1990s, wearing sports gear was cool, even if you weren't sporty. Tracksuits, trainers and sweatshirts were popular, made by companies such as Nike® and Adidas®.

2000s

Clothes by top designers and models were available for the first time in many high-street shops (left). Cheaper stores, such as Primark, became popular as people looked for bargains.

DESIGNER DIVAS

You might have seen their clothes in glossy magazines and on TV, but what are fashion designers really like? Here's the low-down on three of fashion's most famous names.

STELLA McCARTNEY

Stella was born in London and graduated from art college in 1995. She became Creative Director at Paris fashion house, Chloé, in 1997. In 2001, Stella launched her own fashion house and showed her first collection. She never uses fur or leather in her designs.

MANISH MALHOTRA

Manish, India's leading designer, began his fashion career making fabulous costumes for Bollywood movies. In 1998, he branched out into mainstream markets and had his first fashion show. His clothes, such as those modelled here, feature classic Indian **embroidered** designs blended with modern fabrics.

JIMMY CHOO

Malaysian-born Jimmy Choo went to fashion college, before setting up a workshop in London in 1986. In 1988 his designs first featured in top fashion magazine, *Vogue*. Now he specialises in designing luxury, hand-made shoes for women. Their classic but glamorous design makes them a favourite with celebrities.

PUTTING ON A SHOW

The best way for designers to get their latest collections noticed is to showcase them at fashion shows. But getting your clothes to the catwalk **(also called a runway) takes months of hard work. Here's a look behind-the-scenes...**

"Hi, my name's Elle, and I'm a stylist at a big fashion house. I'm part of a big team, working on getting everything ready for a fashion show. Here's my blog...

Six months to go...
We're going to show our new summer collection. It's full of tropical designs and bold colours. Gorgeous! But now the hard work really begins.

Five months to go...
We've been checking out the venue, and sorting the lighting, catwalk set-up and music. Our theme is 'Island Summer' and we're going for a blend of African influences.

Four months to go…
The last month has been crazy. While the clothes are being made, we've been picking the models. It's really important to get the whole look exactly right. The fittings start next week.

Eight weeks to go…
It's getting really scary now. There's still so much to do. I've been busy sending out invites to fashion buyers, editors and other designers. Oh, and to some special celeb guests.

The week before…
What a week! One of our models fell ill so we had to find a last-minute replacement. We've had a lighting and music test, plus sorted out the final running order. Let's hope nothing else goes wrong…

http://www.modeaparis.com

WEBtag Home of Paris Fashion Week – includes designers' links.

The day before…
The dress rehearsal went okay, with just a few problems to sort out. It's not just the models who need to know what to do, like practising all their changes of clothes. It's also the whole team of dressers, make-up artists and hair stylists backstage.

On the day…
Well, it's here – the day of the show! We're all too busy to be nervous. Wish us luck!

Afterwards…
Everything went BRILLIANTLY! People loved the clothes. We've already had lots of orders so we're going to be very busy. And there's the next fashion show to plan!

You can watch fashion shows all over the world, but the most important ones are held in Paris, London, Milan and New York.

http://www.mbfashion week.com/newyork

WEBtag Home of New York Fashion Week, with links to *Daily* magazine.

THIN MODELS

Models are the face of fashion, appearing on catwalks, in photos for magazines and newspapers, and in TV adverts. They usually sign up with a modelling agency who helps them to find work.

Many people criticise the fashion industry for using ultra-skinny models. They're called 'size zero' models (that's the smallest clothes size sold in US stores). What do you think, are you for them or against them?

FOR...

The fashion industry is all about selling clothes. Clothes look better on slim models. Slim models also look better in photographs.

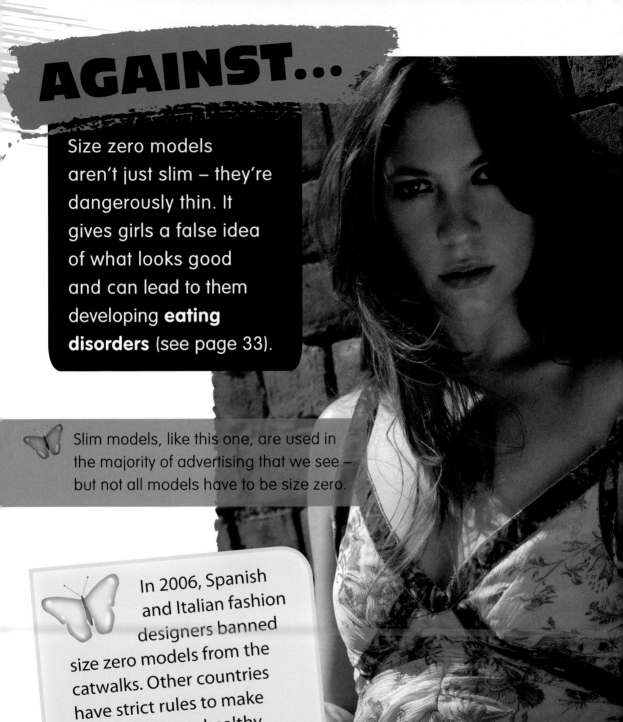

AGAINST...

Size zero models aren't just slim – they're dangerously thin. It gives girls a false idea of what looks good and can lead to them developing **eating disorders** (see page 33).

Slim models, like this one, are used in the majority of advertising that we see – but not all models have to be size zero.

In 2006, Spanish and Italian fashion designers banned size zero models from the catwalks. Other countries have strict rules to make sure models are healthy.

http://www.disordered-eating.co.uk/index.html

WEBtag More information on the size zero debate, plus information, support and videos about eating disorders.

PHOTOSHOP FAKES

Fashion magazines are full of photos of models with fabulous figures, glossy hair and glowing skin. But are they really as perfect as they look? You might be surprised. Look at the differences between these two photos.

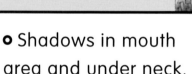

- Shadows in mouth area and under neck.
- Freckles/spots on face, back and arm.
- Blonde hair dull and limp.
- Greasy, shiny nose.
- Distracting wording on hat band.
- Eyes look tired and dark.

The photo on the right has been altered to make the model look as good as possible. Images are 'airbrushed' using computer software, such as Adobe® Photoshop®, to make a model's teeth whiter, lips fuller and skin clearer.

WEBtag Some of the basic techniques used to alter images using Photoshop®.

http://tutorialblog.org/photo-retouching-tutorial-roundup

o Spots, freckles, and text on hat removed with **spot healing brush**.
o Image colour boosted by increasing colour **saturation** levels; hair appears brighter.
o Image blurred to focus on model's eyes.
o Eyes brightened.

So, is airbrushing photos okay? Or does it give a totally false picture?

GET THE RIGHT FIT

With so many clothes to choose from, how do you know what's going to look good on you?

Before you do anything, focus on you! What's your body shape, your skin colour, hair, height and size?
Keep these things in mind when you shop, and use these key steps to find the perfect fit:

- Always try clothes on in the store. It sounds obvious, but whatever your body size, label sizes vary from store to store, so check first.

- Don't buy a smaller size hoping you'll be able to squeeze into it later. Be honest with yourself!

- Jeans: tight is cool, but it has to be right. See how they look when you sit or bend down – not just when you're standing up.

- Go shopping with people whose opinions you value and trust.

- Prepare well for big parties and prom night. Don't leave it until the last minute to find the perfect dress – especially if you want to hire one.

- Don't forget accessories, such as belts, bags and necklaces. These can add style to older outfits.

Your body shape

Your shape will change as you get older, and vary depending on your **diet** and how much exercise you do. Try to buy clothes to suit your body shape. But it doesn't matter what shape you are – just enjoy being you.

pear   cornet   hourglass   lollipop   bell

ARE YOU A FASHION DISASTER?

Are you a style success or a fashion disaster?
Try this quick quiz to find out how you and
your friends shape up.

1 What comes
first when you're
choosing clothes?

A They're comfortable

B They're stylish

2 For you, dressing
up means...

A Jeans and a T-shirt

B Sparkly dress

3 What's your
idea of casual?

A Pyjamas **B** Jeans and a T-shirt

4 What's the worst
item you've ever bought?

A A top from a charity shop

B A designer top you
only wore once

5 Which outfit wouldn't you be seen dead in?

A I'd wear anything

B Something from last year

6 How do you describe your own style?

A Thrown together

B Casual **chic**

Answers – if you chose…

Mostly As
Fashion disaster
Oops! Your wardrobe's a disaster area. Have a good clear out and start all over again. But take someone shopping with you. You can't be trusted on your own.

Mostly Bs
Style success
Congratulations! You're a natural who has a way with clothes and always looks totally cool. You know just what to wear and just when to wear it.

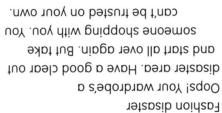

Just because something's in fashion doesn't mean it's going to look good. If you don't like the latest trend, don't wear it. Find your own individual style, and have fun.

http://ellegirl.elle.com

WEBtag Get fashion ideas here at *Elle Girl* magazine online.

HAIRCARE

Fancy changing your hairstyle? Want hair that looks great? Our beauty expert, Hannah, is here to answer your haircare questions.

Q How often should I wash my hair?

Hannah says: Everyone's hair is different. If it's greasy, you might want to wash it regularly – but not every day. Find a shampoo that's suited to your hair type (greasy, fine, dry, etc).

Q Do I need to use a conditioner?

Hannah says: You don't need to, but it makes hair feel smoother – so it's easier to comb or brush. If your hair feels sticky after using conditioner, try a different sort, or just use it on the ends of your hair.

Q How can I fix split ends?

Hannah says: Split ends are a sign of wear and tear, and can't be fixed. You'll have to get your hairdresser to trim them off.

DID YOU KNOW?
Split ends, or trichoptilosis, occur when the protective outer layer of hair is damaged, causing the hair to split into strands. Split ends are caused by blow drying, over-washing and using straighteners.

Q What kind of hairbrush should I use?

Hannah says: A flat, paddle-shaped brush is good for brushing out hair and blow-drying hair smooth. To blow-dry hair in waves or curls, use a round brush.

Q I want to change my hairstyle? What do I do?

Hannah says: Look in magazines or on websites for a style you like. Then take a picture to your hairdresser. He or she will be able to tell you if it suits your face shape. If not, they can advise you on a cool new style that will work.

MAKE-UP MAKEOVER

It can be fun experimenting with make-up, as long as you don't end up looking like a clown!

Choose colours that suit your eye colour and skin tone. And make sure you wash it off at night. Of course, you don't have to wear make-up if you prefer the natural look.

My make-up bag

○ Eyeliner
Ancient Egyptians drew thick lines around their eyes.

○ Make-up brushes
Wash these in warm soapy water regularly to kill nasty **bacteria**.

○ Lipstick or lip gloss
First worn by people in ancient India – when it was made by crushing plants and beetles!

○ Eyeshadow
Add drama to your eyes by using bold colours.

Mascara

Invented by Eugene Rimmel in the 19th century.

Blusher

Also called *rouge*, it's used to highlight cheekbones.

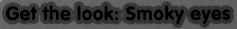

Get the look: Smoky eyes

1. Use your finger or a make-up brush to apply a light colour under your brow bone.
2. Apply a darker colour to your eye socket.
3. Blend in the edges of the colours with your finger so there are no hard lines.
4. Draw a line of eyeliner under your bottom lashes and above your top lashes.
5. Apply mascara to finish the look.

1
2
3
4
5

Don't keep make up for too long – always check for a use-by date. For example, mascara lasts for only six months. Otherwise, harmful bacteria can start to build up.

www.lorealparis.co.uk/beautyconfidential

WEBtag Features a video gallery of beauty tips from a top make-up artist.

GOOD SKIN GUIDE

Don't let bad skin days cramp your style. Follow our top tips for keeping your skin in great condition.

Top skincare tips

o Wash your face twice a day: in the morning and at night. Use a mild, unperfumed soap or a gentle facial scrub.

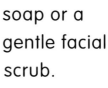

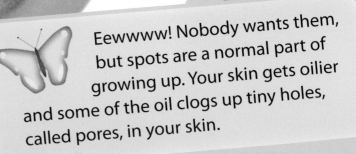

Eewwww! Nobody wants them, but spots are a normal part of growing up. Your skin gets oilier and some of the oil clogs up tiny holes, called pores, in your skin.

○ Use a moisturiser after you've washed your face. It'll keep your skin soft and supple. Find one to match your skin type.

○ Eat a healthy diet and drink lots of water – it's brilliant for your skin.

WEBtag Loads of fashion and beauty tips from this on-line magazine.

http://www.cosmogirl.com

○ If you get spots, don't keep touching your face. You'll transfer bacteria and dirt from your fingers to your face and make spots worse.

○ Never pick or squeeze spots. Try one of the spot treatments you can buy from the chemist's.

○ As a special treat, try a face mask (above). There are lots of different kinds, but cucumber and avocado are especially skin-friendly.

○ In summer, always wear **sunscreen** with a high sun protection factor (spf 30) on your face – and other parts in direct sunlight!

DIET DISTRESS

When people say they're 'on a diet', they mean they're trying to lose weight by eating less.

You and your friends might wonder if you should go on diets, too. But you probably don't need too. Being overweight can be unhealthy, but diets can be just as bad for you. Eating too little or skipping meals can stop your body growing properly.

Shop models like these all tend to be a standard size. Humans aren't like this, each of us is **unique**.

WEBtag Eating disorder charity webpages for young people.

http://www.b-eat.co.uk/YoungPeople/Home

EATING DISORDERS

Some people worry so much about food and eating that they make themselves ill. They may have an eating disorder, such as **anorexia** or **bulimia**.

SHOCKING RESULTS

A 2010 survey by *Bliss* magazine revealed that nine out of ten teenage girls in the UK were unhappy with their body. Of 2,000 girls, 19% said they had suffered from an eating disorder.

Important note from Anita:
If you think you, or anyone else you know, might have an eating disorder, tell someone you trust. The sooner you or your friend get help, the sooner you'll get better.

HEALTHY EATING

Eating a good diet is essential for keeping your body in peak condition. And it's easier than you think. Here are five tasty tips for healthy eating...

Try to make time for breakfast – even if it means getting up a little earlier.

○ Don't skip breakfast. Your energy supplies need topping up after you've been asleep.
○ Swap unhealthy snacks, such as crisps and biscuits, for healthy snacks, like fruit.

http://www.youngwomens
health.org/healthyeating.html

WEBtag More tips on how to stay healthy from the Center for Young Women's Health.

o Eat when you're hungry, but stop eating when you're full.

o Pick freshly-cooked food over junk food which is high in sugar, salt and fat.

o Drink plenty of water – around six glasses a day.

 Try cooking with fresh ingredients – your friends might even help out.

What's on your plate?

1 Fruit and vegetables: eat at least five portions a day.

2 Bread, cereals, potatoes: eat lots for energy.

3 Meat, fish, eggs, pulses, milk and dairy: eat medium amounts to help you grow.

4 Fatty and sugary foods: eat the smallest amounts of these.

GET IT, FEEL FABULOUS!

Exercise is good for you – it's official! But it doesn't have to be a hard slog. Choose a sport or activity you enjoy and you're more likely to stick at it. Oh, and playing computer games doesn't count!

Check out these activities – we've also added the calorie burn too.

(Person weighing 50kg; moderate activity; 30 minutes.)

Calories refer to the amount of energy in food. Different types of food have higher or lower calorie levels. Our bodies 'burn' calories, especially when we are active.

Dancing –
151 calories.

Cycling –
100 calories.

Football –
178 calories.

Running –
215 calories.

Sweet dreams

Feeling tired and worn out? Perhaps you're not getting enough Zzzzzzzs. Sleep is vital for letting your body rest and recover after a busy day. Skimping on sleep can leave you feeling and looking dreadful. Between the ages of 8–10, you need around 10 hours' sleep a night. This goes down to around 9 hours when you're 11–15 years old.

If you're having trouble dropping off, forget counting sheep. Have a warm, relaxing bath, or read for a while before you go to bed. Watching TV or doing exercise will keep you awake.

Horse riding –
164 calories.

Swimming –
154 calories.

Martial arts –
255 calories.

http://www.teengrowth.com

THE PRICE OF FASHION

Today, you don't have to head to an expensive boutique or spend a fortune to look good. Stores and supermarkets stock clothes and accessories that aren't just stylish, they're also cheap.

Sounds good, but what about the hidden costs?

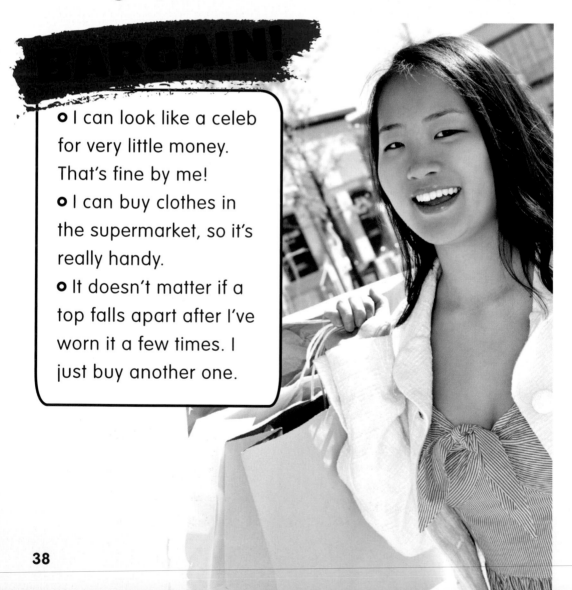

BARGAIN!

- I can look like a celeb for very little money. That's fine by me!
- I can buy clothes in the supermarket, so it's really handy.
- It doesn't matter if a top falls apart after I've worn it a few times. I just buy another one.

Conditions in sweatshops can be harsh – with no toilet breaks or talking allowed.

STITCH UP!

o The clothes are cheap because they're made in poor countries, such as Vietnam and Bangladesh, where people are paid low wages.

o In the clothing factories, called sweatshops, people work long hours in poor conditions.

o Sometimes, the workers are young children because they're cheaper to employ.

DID YOU KNOW?
Some garment workers in Bangladesh earn as little as £8 a month for working 80 hours a week in a sweatshop. They can be beaten or sacked if they refuse to work overtime.

http://www.cleanclothes.org

WEBtag Anti-sweatshop news from the Clean Clothes Campaign.

CELEBRITY SLIP-UPS

If you've had a wardrobe disaster, don't stress out. You're not alone! Even the best-dressed celebs suffer a major style slip-up from time to time. Here are some famous ones...

Oh dear, Emma Watson. We're not loving the nightie look.

No, no, no, Geri Halliwell. We don't want to see your pants.

Looks like Lily Allen's left half her dress at home.

These wardrobe disasters could have been avoided. Follow the **MY ZONE** guide for fault-free party clothing:

FAULT-FREE CLOTHING GUIDE

○ Try your outfit on before your big night to make sure it all works together.

○ Ask your mum's opinion – it's a good way to avoid a massive argument later!

○ Make sure you dress for the occasion; ask your friends what they plan to wear.

○ If you choose to wear new or high-heel shoes, make sure you get used to wearing them before you go out.

Is Selma Hayek wearing her granny's old carpet? We think so.

Is it an ostrich? No, it's Madonna, and she should know better.

YOU'RE HIRED!

**Want to work in fashion? Think you can cut it?
Here are some of the jobs you might like to try.**

1 BOUTIQUE MANAGER

Job description:
You're responsible for the day-to-day running of a shop. You choose the right clothes to sell and make sure the shop is clean, tidy and well organised.

Above all, you need to keep your customers happy, especially if they're asking for fashion advice.

2 FASHION PHOTOGRAPHER

Job description:

Your job is to take the photos that appear in fashion magazines, newspapers and adverts, and to photograph fashion shows. Apart from having a **creative eye**, you'll also be good with gadgets because you'll be working with top-of-the-range camera equipment.

3 PATTERN CUTTER

Job description:

You'll turn a designer's sketch into a working pattern that can be used for making a garment.

4 FASHION BUYER

Job description:

You'll be hired by shops to buy in ranges of clothing, shoes and accessories. You'll need to know what's in, what's out and what's going to be hot next season.

5 FASHION JOURNALIST

Job description:

You'll research and write articles for magazines, newspapers and the Internet. If you're good enough, you might even become a magazine editor, like Alexandra Shulman (left), editor of British *Vogue*.

43

GLOSSARY

Anorexia – an eating disorder where sufferers eat so little that they are starving their body, yet they still believe that they are fat.

Bacteria – tiny organisms, some of which are known as germs, which can cause diseases.

Bulimia – an eating disorder where sufferers binge on food (eat a lot), then make themselves sick to get rid of it so that they don't put on weight.

Catwalk – a narrow walkway that models walk along during a fashion show. The audience sits on either side of the catwalk.

Chic – stylish and elegant.

Creative eye – being able to work out which patterns, styles and colours go together, or how to position models and lighting well.

Diet – the food you eat every day. Going on a diet usually means that you cut down on certain foods or the amount of food you eat to lose weight.

Eating disorders – food-related illnesses, such as anorexia and bulimia, that affect people who are worried about their body image.

Embroidered – when a piece of fabric has been decorated with a needlework pattern.

Fashion house – the company of a famous fashion designer.

Garment – a piece of clothing.

PVC – a stretchy, plastic material. Its full name is polyvinyl chloride.

Saturation (colour) – colour intensity and richness.

Seasonal – clothes that are styled or suited to the seasons – spring, summer, autumn and winter.

Spot healing brush – Photoshop® graphics tool used to remove marks from digital images.

Style – the way in which clothes and accessories are worn, or another way of describing what is in fashion at a particular time.

Sunscreen – cream or lotion that contains chemicals which reflect some of the Sun's damaging rays.

Trendsetters – people who create a new fashion that other people copy or follow.

Unique – being the only one of a particular type.

MORE WEBSITES

**http://www.bbc.co.uk/
blast/fashion**

This BBC website features fashion advice, videos
and a 'how to' section so you can get creative.

http://fashionista.com

Super-stylish website from Stella McCartney which includes
fashion news, careers advice, plus style and beauty tips.

http://www.bbc.co.uk/switch/slink

The Slink website, featuring a section on hair and beauty
tips, beauty lab and fashion videos.

http://www.sugarscape.com

Website of teen magazine *Sugar*, with
fashion, beauty and celebrity news.

http://www.canucutit.co.uk

Can U Cut It In Fashion website, with
lots of careers-based information,
including top tips from
fashion industry
professionals.

INDEX